# EVOLVE

## WORKBOOK

Mari Vargo

# 6B

CAMBRIDGE
UNIVERSITY PRESS

# CAMBRIDGE
## UNIVERSITY PRESS

University Printing House, Cambridge CB2 8BS, United Kingdom

One Liberty Plaza, 20th Floor, New York, NY 10006, USA

477 Williamstown Road, Port Melbourne, VIC 3207, Australia

314–321, 3rd Floor, Plot 3, Splendor Forum, Jasola District Centre, New Delhi – 110025, India

79 Anson Road, #06–04/06, Singapore 079906

Cambridge University Press is part of the University of Cambridge.

It furthers the University's mission by disseminating knowledge in the pursuit of education, learning and research at the highest international levels of excellence.

www.cambridge.org
Information on this title: www.cambridge.org/9781108411967

First published 2020

20  19  18  17  16  15  14  13  12  11  10  9  8  7  6  5  4  3  2  1

Printed in the United Kingdom by Latimer Trend

*A catalogue record for this publication is available from the British Library*

ISBN  978-1-108-40535-5  Student's Book
ISBN  978-1-108-40514-0  Student's Book A
ISBN  978-1-108-40931-5  Student's Book B
ISBN  978-1-108-40537-9  Student's Book with Practice Extra
ISBN  978-1-108-40515-7  Student's Book with Practice Extra A
ISBN  978-1-108-40932-2  Student's Book with Practice Extra B
ISBN  978-1-108-40909-4  Workbook with Audio
ISBN  978-1-108-40885-1  Workbook with Audio A
ISBN  978-1-108-41196-7  Workbook with Audio B
ISBN  978-1-108-40520-1  Teacher's Edition with Test Generator
ISBN  978-1-108-41077-9  Presentation Plus
ISBN  978-1-108-41206-3  Class Audio CDs
ISBN  978-1-108-40802-8  Video Resource Book with DVD
ISBN  978-1-108-41451-7  Full Contact with DVD
ISBN  978-1-108-41157-8  Full Contact with DVD A
ISBN  978-1-108-41424-1  Full Contact with DVD B

Additional resources for this publication at www.cambridge.org/evolve

# CONTENTS

# UNIT 7 ROOTS

## 7.1 IT'S IN THE BLOOD

### 1 VOCABULARY: Talking about ancestry

A **Match the words with the definitions.**

| | | | | |
|---|---|---|---|---|
| 1 | adopt | _b_ | a | the study of the history of a person's family |
| 2 | adoption | ___ | b | to legally make someone else's child part of your own family |
| 3 | adoptive | ___ | c | relating to the way traits are passed from parents to children |
| 4 | ancestral | ___ | d | relating to a family member from any time in the past |
| 5 | ancestor | ___ | e | the fact of belonging to a cultural or national group |
| 6 | ancestry | ___ | f | to be born with a family member's characteristics |
| 7 | ethnic | ___ | g | the process of getting legal permission to raise someone's child |
| 8 | ethnicity | ___ | h | relating to cultural or national origins |
| 9 | genealogy | ___ | i | traditions and other features belonging to a culture |
| 10 | genes | ___ | j | a member of your family from any time in the past |
| 11 | genetic | ___ | k | the long line of people who came before you |
| 12 | hereditary | ___ | l | the characteristics of a person inherited from parents |
| 13 | heritage | ___ | m | related, especially as parents of someone, through adoption |
| 14 | inherit | ___ | n | relating to the qualities we inherit from our ancestors |

B **Check (✓) the correct sentences. Then correct the mistakes in the incorrect sentences.**

1 I sent off a DNA sample to find out about my ~~genealogy~~ *genetic* history. ☐

2 Before I sent it, I didn't know much about my ethnic. ☐

3 I'm adopted, and I don't know much about my biological parents. ☐

4 My adoption parents never met my biological parents. ☐

5 I found out that most of my ancestors were from Mongolia. ☐

6 Now I'm trying to learn as much as possible about my Mongolian hereditary. ☐

7 Looking at pictures of people from Mongolia, I can see that I probably inherited a lot of my features from my Mongolian ancestors. ☐

### 2 GRAMMAR: Negative and limiting adverbials

A <u>Underline</u> the negative and limiting adverbials.

1 Never had I imagined that I might be 23% Eastern European.

2 Only when I asked my father did I find out that his grandparents were from Russia.

3 Not until I had children did I become interested in genealogy.

4 Only when I had discovered more about my genetic makeup did I want to find out who my ancestors were.

5 Little did I know my great grandparents were from Tokyo.

**B** **Put the words in the correct order to make sentences. Add a form of *do* when necessary.**

1 I would / South America / to find / be able / relatives / in / never / I / think

   <u>Never did I think I would be able to find relatives in</u>
   <u>South America.</u>

2 from my / I / realize / little / grandmother / I inherited / my freckles

   _____

   _____

3 would / had an aunt / never / towns away / guessed / that I / I have / living two

   _____

   _____

4 tell me / my mother / only when / I asked / that I'm / part Irish

   _____

5 I sent in / a DNA sample / Asian ancestry / not until / I know / that I have

   _____

6 without using / have found / no way / my cousins / a DNA ancestry kit / would / I

   _____

**C** **Circle the correct words and phrases to complete the sentences.**

1 *Not until / Never* would I have imagined that I was related to a famous singer.

2 *Little / Not until* I met my grandfather did I know who I inherited my height from.

3 *Little / Only* did I know I'm not actually Spanish at all.

4 *Only when / Not until* my friend suggested getting a DNA test did I even consider it.

5 *Not until / No way* would I have considered getting a DNA test before my friend did his.

## 3 GRAMMAR AND VOCABULARY

**A** **Complete the stories with the words in parentheses and your own ideas.**

1 My whole life I thought I was 100% Italian. Imagine my shock when I found some relatives online and found out that my mother's great grandparents were Chinese! No way (ancestors)

   _____.

2 I grew up learning all about Italian culture. I didn't know anything about Chinese culture. Not until (heritage)

   _____.

3 My mother didn't believe me when I told her about what I had discovered, so I showed her the genealogy record that my relatives sent me. Only when (ancestry)

   _____.

4 I did some more research and found out that we also have roots in Sweden. We always wondered who my little brother inherited his blond hair and blue eyes from. Little (genes)

   _____.

# 7.2  A VERY SPECIAL OCCASION

## 1  VOCABULARY: Talking about customs and traditions

**A**  Complete the chart with the words in the box.

| festivities | honor (our grandmother) | keep alive | mark (the occasion) |
|---|---|---|---|
| observe | pay tribute to | (this) practice | rites |
| ritual | significance | signify | symbolize |

| Nouns | Verbs |
|---|---|
|  |  |
|  |  |

**B**  Circle the correct words to complete the story.

Every year, my family gets together to ¹*honor / observe* the holiday of *Chuseok*, a Korean harvest celebration. The ²*festivities / practices* take place during the eighth month of the lunar year when there's a full moon.

We always prepare a lot of delicious foods for *Chuseok*. The abundance of food ³*signifies / honors* a good harvest. One of these foods is *seongpyeon*, a type of rice cake. It is white, shaped like a half circle, and filled with things like sesame seeds or pine nuts. Because of its shape, it ⁴*marks / symbolizes* the moon.

Ancestors are also an important part of *Chuseok*. First, we have a memorial service at home. This ⁵*significance / ritual* usually takes place in the morning. Then we visit our ancestors' graves later in the day to *observe / honor* them.

My family and I participate in Chuseok because we really enjoy it, but more importantly, we do it because we want to help ⁶*keep / mark* these traditions ⁷*significant / alive*.

## 2  GRAMMAR: Fronting adverbials

**A**  Complete the sentences. Match 1–5 with a–e.

1  On the table _____d_____        **a**  people are talking and having fun.

2  From the kitchen _____        **b**  float sounds of raindrops falling.

3  Around the house _____        **c**  is bread baking to a golden-brown color.

4  Through the window _____        **d**  lay plates full of traditional foods.

5  In the oven _____        **e**  come sounds of cooking and laughing.

B   **Check (✓) the correct sentences. Then correct the mistakes in the incorrect sentences.**

                  *people cook*

1   In the kitchen ~~cook people~~ traditional foods.  ☐

2   Throughout the house we put up decorations.  ☐

3   From the living room coming the sounds of the television.  ☐

4   On the walls hang we pictures of our ancestors.  ☐

5   From the backyard float the sounds of children playing.  ☐

C   **Bring the adverbials in bold to the front of each sentence. Make any changes to word order that are needed.**

1   The sound of a fire crackling comes **from the fireplace**.

    *From the fireplace comes the sound of a fire crackling.*

2   Adults and children are hanging decorations **around the house**.

3   Sounds of music and chatter come **from the kitchen**.

4   Delicious scents of cooking waft **throughout the house**.

5   Traditional dishes are **in the oven** roasting.

6   A beautiful vase of flowers sits **on the table**.

## 3 GRAMMAR AND VOCABULARY

A   **Think about a celebration or event. Complete the sentences with your own ideas. Use words from the box in at least three of your sentences.**

| rites | keep alive | observe | mark | festivities | ritual |
|---|---|---|---|---|---|
| significance | honor | symbolize | pay tribute to | practice | signify |

1   In the kitchen _____ .

2   On the table _____ .

3   From the living room _____ .

4   Through the kitchen door _____ .

5   Around the house _____ .

# 7.3 THE STORY OF A RETURNEE

## 1 LISTENING

**A** 🔊 **7.01** **LISTEN FOR ATTITUDE** How did the following things affect Elsa? Match each part of her experience with the correct attitude.

1 speaking German _____
2 meeting all her relatives _____
3 staying at her aunt's house _____

a overwhelmed
b happy
c anxious

**B** 🔊 **7.01** **DEDUCE MEANING** Look at the words and phrases from the conversation. What do they mean? Listen again and use context clues to help you figure out the meanings.

1 tongue-tied
   a talking too much     b unable to speak     c having a sore throat

2 gibberish
   a meaningful words     b a specific language     c words that don't make sense

3 keeping everyone straight
   a remembering who is who     b having people stand in line     c being very serious with people

4 fried
   a overcooked     b energetic     c exhausted

5 anticipated
   a excited     b expected     c wondered

6 hit it off
   a got to know each other     b got into a fight     c got along well

**C** 🔊 **7.01** **LISTEN FOR DETAILS** Listen again and read the statements about Elsa. Write *T* (true) or *F* (false).

1 She was nervous before she got to Germany. _____
2 She went to Germany alone. _____
3 She doesn't speak any German. _____
4 She met over 100 people at the reunion. _____
5 She remembers everyone's name. _____
6 She stayed at her grandparents' house. _____
7 She enjoyed meeting two of her cousins. _____
8 Her cousins are almost the same age as she is. _____
9 She is going to visit her cousins again next summer. _____
10 Her mother visits her sister in Germany once a year. _____

## 2 CRITICAL THINKING

**A** **THINK CRITICALLY** What do you think Elsa learned from having gone to her family reunion in Germany?

_____

_____

## 3 SPEAKING

**A** **Read the expressions. Write _C_ (commenting on your own story), _E_ (expressing an opinion), or _R_ (responding to someone else's story).**

1  I can see how it would be strange. ____
2  To tell you the truth, … ____
3  How did you handle that? ____

4  It's difficult to say why, exactly. ____
5  It's hard to describe. ____
6  Don't get me wrong, … ____

**B** **Put the conversation in the correct order.**

____ **Elsa** That was the weirdest part! I look so much like all these people I'd never met before.

_1_ **Max** How was the food at the reunion? Was it as good as your mom's?

____ **Elsa** To tell you the truth, it helped me feel like part of the family.

____ **Max** I think I can understand that. So, did you see a family resemblance between you and any of your relatives?

____ **Elsa** I have to admit, it was even better than my mom's. It was delicious. I got some recipes from my aunt. I'll make one of the dishes for you.

____ **Elsa** It was beautiful. It's difficult to put into words, but I really felt the history of the place. There are so many old buildings there. In some places, I felt like I'd stepped back in time, if you know what I mean.

____ **Max** I can see how that would be strange. Did it make you feel uncomfortable?

____ **Max** I can't wait to try it. How did you like Germany in general?

**C** **Imagine that you took a trip like Elsa's. Complete the conversation with your own ideas.**

**A**  How was your trip to _____ ?

**B**  To tell you the truth, _____ .

**A**  It must have been pretty overwhelming. Did you like the food?

**B**  That was the best part! _____ .

**A**  That sounds great. Did you enjoy meeting your family members?

**B**  Well, I was really nervous. It's difficult to say why exactly, but _____ .

# WHEN A LANGUAGE DIES

## 1 READING

A **READ THE MAIN IDEA** Read the article below. Then (circle) the main idea.

   **a** It is impossible for one person to successfully create a new language.

   **b** It is important to preserve languages that are disappearing.

   **c** Constructed languages might prove that language affects thought.

B **READ FOR ATTITUDE** Read the article again. Is the writer emotionally engaged? Why do you think so?

### What Can We Learn from Constructed Languages?

One argument for saving disappearing languages is the idea that when we lose a language, we lose a way of thinking. Can language affect, or even control, the way we think? Examining constructed languages – those created by a single person or group of people – shows us that our thoughts might be limited by the words we use.

Many people may be familiar with languages invented for TV shows, such as *Star Trek* (Klingon) and *Game of Thrones* (Dothraki). However, hundreds of languages have been constructed. One of these is Newspeak, which was invented by author George Orwell for his novel *1984*. In the novel, the rulers of Oceania create Newspeak, based on English, in order to control their citizens. One way that they achieve this is by limiting vocabulary. With a greatly reduced vocabulary, citizens don't have the words to express complex thoughts, and the rulers hope this will stop them from actually *having* complex thoughts.

Another language that attempts to affect thought is E-Prime. Also based on English, E-Prime has only one special rule – it doesn't include any form of the verb *be*. Because the verb *be* is used so frequently in English, this simple change requires speakers to be more creative and more precise with their speech. For example, instead of saying "That's a terrible idea," an E-Prime speaker has to say something like, "I don't think that idea will work."

Newspeak and E-Prime are two examples of languages that were created with the goal of influencing thought and expression. One attempts to limit thought and the other tries to expand it. Would they have influenced people's thoughts if they were actually widely spoken? Those who argue that thought creates language might say no. However, I believe that it's the other way around—language creates thought.

## 2 CRITICAL THINKING

A **THINK CRITICALLY** Do you agree with the writer's conclusion? Why or why not?

_____

_____

_____

_____

_____

_____

_____

_____

## 3 WRITING

A **Read the summary of the text. Has the writer captured the main idea and argument correctly? <u>Underline</u> any incorrect information. Is there any key information missing?**

The constructed languages Newspeak and E-Prime show us that language can affect thought. Newspeak does this by restricting vocabulary. In addition, it restricts the use of the verb *be* so that speakers have to be creative in order to express their ideas. E-Prime, which is based on English, aims to make speakers and writers use more precise language, thereby influencing the way they think. Some say that thought influences language. However, Newspeak and E-Prime show us that language might, in fact, control thought.

B **Rewrite the end of the summary in exercise 3A using one of the parallel structures below.**

Some argue that … but the author disagrees, saying …

While some say … , the author feels …

Many claim that … However, the author maintains that …

_____

_____

C **Rewrite the summary in exercise 3A. Make sure that it captures the main idea and argument correctly and that there's no key information missing.**

_____

_____

_____

_____

_____

# CHECK AND REVIEW

**Read the statements. Can you do these things?**

| UNIT 7 | Mark the boxes.  ☑ I can do it.  ? I am not sure. I can … | | If you are not sure, go back to these pages in the Student's Book. |
|---|---|---|---|
| VOCABULARY | ☐ talk about ancestry. | | page 66 |
| | ☐ talk about customs and traditions. | | page 68 |
| GRAMMAR | ☐ use negative and limiting adverbials. | | page 67 |
| | ☐ use fronting adverbials. | | page 69 |
| LISTENING AND SPEAKING SKILLS | ☐ listen to a podcast and deduce meaning from context clues. | | page 70 |
| | ☐ comment on my own story, express an opinion, and respond to someone else's story. | | page 71 |
| READING AND WRITING SKILLS | ☐ identify bias in an article. | | page 73 |
| | ☐ write a summary with a concluding statement. | | page 73 |

# 8.1 THE ATTENTION SPAN MYTH

## 1 VOCABULARY: Talking about attention and distraction

A Complete the chart with the correct form of each word.

| Nouns | Verbs |
|---|---|
| concentration | |
| | distract |
| focus | |
| | interrupt |

B Complete the phrases with the words in the box.

~~distracted~~    distractions    focus    focused    interrupted

1 be / get _____*distracted*_____
2 be / get _____
3 get / stay _____
4 lose _____
5 avoid _____

C Complete the sentences with words from exercise 1A. Include the words *by* and *on* when necessary. For some items, more than one answer may be possible.

1 It's hard to get back to work after a(n) _____*interruption*_____ .
2 I can't study in coffee shops because I get _____ by the people around me.
3 I try not to _____ people when they're busy working.
4 Do you find it difficult to _____ on work when people are talking?
5 I avoid _____ by closing my office door.

## 2 GRAMMAR: Phrases with *get*

A Check (✓) the correct sentences. Then correct the mistakes in the incorrect sentences.

1 It's hard for me to get ~~focus~~ *focused* in a noisy room. ☐
2 The article got me wondered about my own attention span. ☐
3 I'm getting annoyed by all the distractions. ☐
4 I can't get my work finish in this environment. ☐
5 The conversation got thinking about the distractions I deal with every day. ☐
6 I get distracted easily. ☐
7 I'm getting exhaust by all the demands on my attention. ☐
8 Can you help me have this window open? ☐

B **Write sentences using the cues in parentheses.**

1 (I can't / get / anything / do / today)

I can't get anything done today.

2 (your comment yesterday / get / me / think / about my workspace)

3 (right now/ my patience / get / eat away /by constant interruptions)

4 (it's easy / get / distract / around here)

5 (How can you / get / focus / with all these distractions)

6 (yesterday's meeting / get / us / talk / about the future of the company)

## 3 GRAMMAR AND VOCABULARY

A **Complete the sentences with your own ideas.**

1 My ability to concentrate is getting _____ .

2 If I pay attention to all the distractions around me, I can't get _____ .

3 This discussion on ways to improve concentration got _____ .

4 When I have trouble focusing, I get _____ .

# GUT REACTION

## 1 VOCABULARY: Expressions with *get*

**A** **Match the phrases with the definitions.**

get …

| | | | | |
|---|---|---|---|---|
| 1 | accustomed to something | h | **a** | to become irritated and impatient |
| 2 | at | ___ | **b** | to have trouble finding a destination |
| 3 | attached to something | ___ | **c** | to imply something |
| 4 | blown away by something | ___ | **d** | to be amazed by something |
| 5 | complicated | ___ | **e** | to do something correctly |
| 6 | frustrated | ___ | **f** | to throw something away |
| 7 | lost | ___ | **g** | to receive permission to do something |
| 8 | rid of something | ___ | **h** | to get used to something |
| 9 | something right | ___ | **i** | to develop a liking for something |
| 10 | something straight | ___ | **j** | to become problematic or complex |
| 11 | the go-ahead | ___ | **k** | to understand something thoroughly |

**B** Circle **the correct words to complete the conversations.**

1 **A** What happened? You were supposed to be here twenty minutes ago.

   **B** Sorry, I missed the turn for your street and got *the go-ahead /* (*lost*). I had to ask someone for directions.

2 **A** It must be difficult to go from sales associate to manager.

   **B** No, it's great. I'm really getting *accustomed to / frustrated* managing the department.

3 **A** I got *rid of / at* all my old clothes last weekend.

   **B** I have to do that, too. I don't wear most of the things in my closet.

4 **A** Let me get *this right / this straight*. Are you saying that you can speak seven languages?

   **B** Yes, I can!

5 **A** You don't seem excited about moving. I think you're going to love London.

   **B** I am excited, but I'm sad about leaving this apartment. I've lived here for three years, and I've really gotten *blown away by / attached to* it.

6 **A** Have you made the restaurant reservation for Callie's birthday dinner yet?

   **B** No, I'm waiting to get *it right / the go-ahead* from Callie.

**C** THINK CRITICALLY **Think of a time you trusted your instincts. What happened? Were you right or wrong?**

_____

_____

_____

_____

## 2 GRAMMAR: Phrases with *as*

**A** **Put the words in the correct order to form sentences with *as* phrases.**

1 trust yourself / as my / says, / someone else / before / you trust / grandmother

_____

2 more accurate / explains / in his book, / instinct / as Gladwell / can be / than careful consideration

_____

3 instincts all / to follow / it can / the time / as / be difficult / we all know, / your

_____

4 make decisions / half of / say they / as / can be seen / based on instincts / in the graph, / the employees

_____

5 their instincts / as / follow / we / can infer / most participants / from the study,

_____

**B** **Complete the sentences with phrases from the box.**

| all attest | can be | explains | inferred | point out |
|---|---|---|---|---|

1 As _____ seen in the report, it takes about 23 minutes to get back to a task after an interruption.

2 As the article _____ , constant interruptions increase workers' stress.

3 As the researchers _____ , the average office worker switches tasks approximately every five minutes.

4 As we can _____ , it's not possible to concentrate on a difficult task when we're interrupted every few minutes.

5 As can be _____ from the chart, interruptions take up a large amount of an employee's workday.

## 3 GRAMMAR AND VOCABULARY

**A** **Complete the sentences with your own ideas and expressions from the box.**

| get accustomed to | get attached to | get blown away by | get complicated |
|---|---|---|---|
| get frustrated | get lost | get rid of | get something right |

1 As my mother always says, _____ .

2 As you can imagine, _____ .

3 As my teacher points out, _____ .

4 As you can see, _____ .

5 As we can all attest, _____ .

# IT'S THE APP YOU NEED

## 1 LISTENING

A 🔊 **8.01** **LISTEN FOR MAIN POINTS** **Listen to the conversation. What kind of device are Tina and Yuri discussing?**

a one that improves sleep

b one that monitors apps that most distract you

c one that improves concentration

B 🔊 **8.01** **LISTEN FOR DETAILS** **Listen again and write answers to the questions.**

1 What types of disruptions did Yuri have at work?

_____

2 What do the headsets enable users to do?

_____

3 What do the headsets do when a user gets distracted?

_____

4 What is the whole point of the headsets?

_____

5 Why does the app keep a record of a user's concentration patterns?

_____

6 Why does the app play music?

_____

C 🔊 **8.02** **Listen to the sentences and circle the words that you hear.**

1 allow    enable    aim

2 offer    prefer    opportunity

3 goal    bottom    point

4 line    aim    miss

5 market    aim    goals

## 2 CRITICAL THINKING

A  THINK CRITICALLY  **Think of three other ways that Yuri can avoid the kinds of distractions she had at work.**

1 _____
_____

2 _____
_____

3 _____
_____

## 3 SPEAKING

A  **Complete the sentences with the phrases from the box.**

| | | |
|---|---|---|
| bottom line | enables users | goal is |
| great opportunity | miss out | on the market |

1 The app _____ to keep track of tasks.

2 No other app _____ offers as many features.

3 Our _____ to help users get organized.

4 This is a _____ to try the app for free.

5 The _____ is that this is the best organizing app available.

6 You won't want to _____ on this excellent app.

B  **Think of a useful device that you use on a regular basis. Then complete the sentences below to create an advertisement for the device.**

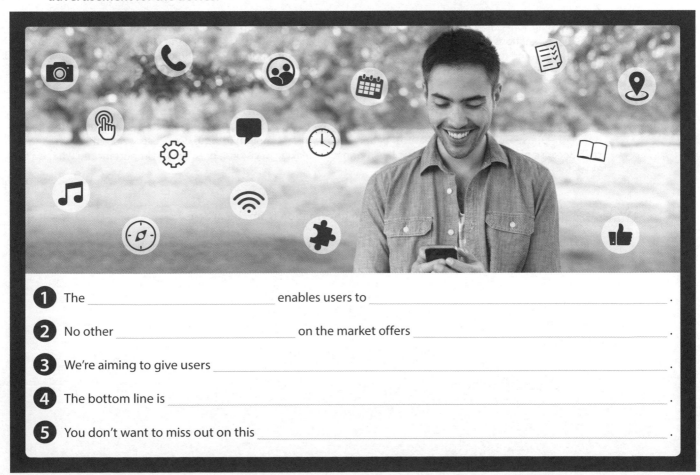

1 The _____ enables users to _____ .

2 No other _____ on the market offers _____ .

3 We're aiming to give users _____ .

4 The bottom line is _____ .

5 You don't want to miss out on this _____ .

# THE PERFECT PITCH

## 1 READING

A Read the article. Write the subheads above the correct paragraphs. You will use only three of the subheads.

| | |
|---|---|
| Sit Down and Summarize | Share Your Knowledge |
| Speed Up Your Reading | Sleep on It |
| Take Breaks | Write It, Don't Type It |

## TIPS FOR BECOMING A QUICK LEARNER

Learning something new can be time consuming, but effectively retaining what you learn, without having to review it multiple times, can shorten the time you spend learning a new skill. Follow these tips for retaining information and learning more quickly.

**1** _____

Pay attention to new information as if you were going to have to teach it to someone else. Approaching new information from a teacher's point of view can help you focus on key points and organize the information into manageable portions even when you are hearing the information for the first time. After you've heard or read the information once, teach it to someone else. That helps you retain what you've learned.

**2** _____

After learning something new, get a good night's sleep. While you sleep, your brain activity doesn't stop. In fact, some brain functions thrive on sleep. For example, research shows that sleep helps the hippocampus, the part of the brain devoted to memory, form long-term memories. Storing information in your long-term memory means you're turning new information into knowledge.

**3** _____

It may be tempting to type your notes on a laptop or tablet, particularly because most of us type faster than we write. However, research reveals that writing things by hand is far superior to typing when it comes to information retention. One reason for this is that most people can't write fast enough to write down every word that someone says. Because of this, we have to process the information, making decisions about what is important and what isn't as we take notes.

B **EVALUATE INFORMATION** Complete the chart with information from the article.

| | Tip 1 | Tip 2 | Tip 3 |
|---|---|---|---|
| **How does following this tip help you learn more quickly?** | | | |

## 2 CRITICAL THINKING

A    **THINK CRITICALLY** Which tip do you think is most useful for you? Why?

_____

_____

_____

_____

## 3 WRITING

A    **Choose the best phrases for slides based on the article.**

**Opening slide:**

1    a    Learn Quickly

      b    You Can Become a Quick Learner

2    a    These tips will help you learn faster

      b    Three tips to speed up your learning

**Tip 1:**

3    a    Learn like a teacher

      b    Try to learn as if you were a teacher

4    a    Focus on key points, retain information

      b    Learning like a teacher helps you focus on and remember the important points

B    **Create presentation slides about Tips 2 and 3 of the article.**

| Tip 2 | Tip 3 |
|---|---|
|  |  |
|  |  |
|  |  |

# CHECK AND REVIEW

**Read the statements. Can you do these things?**

UNIT
8

Mark the boxes.    ✔ I can do it.    ? I am not sure.

If you are not sure, go back to these pages in the Student's Book.

I can …

| | I can … | |
|---|---|---|
| VOCABULARY | ☐ talk about attention and distraction. | page 76 |
| | ☐ use expressions with *get*. | page 78 |
| GRAMMAR | ☐ use phrases with *get*. | page 77 |
| | ☐ use phrases with *as*. | page 79 |
| LISTENING AND SPEAKING SKILLS | ☐ listen for details in a conversation. | page 80 |
| | ☐ use phrases to speak persuasively about a product. | page 81 |
| READING AND WRITING SKILLS | ☐ analyze information in an article. | page 82 |
| | ☐ write presentation slides based on an article. | page 83 |

## 9.1    THE SITTING DISEASE

### 1 VOCABULARY: Discussing health issues

A   **Complete the phrases with words from the box. If a word is not part of a phrase, write an *X* on the line.**

| | | |
|---|---|---|
| cardiovascular | cholesterol | internal |
| pain | pressure | sedentary |
| side | system | |

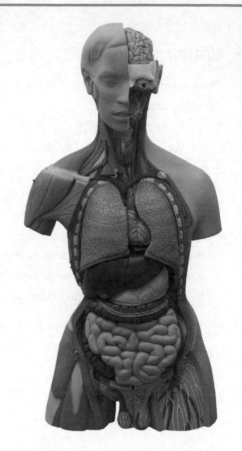

1 _____ effects

2 blood _____

3 posture _____

4 _____ lifestyle

5 immune _____

6 digestion _____

7 joints _____

8 _____ organs

9 _____ disease

10 _____ levels

11 chronic _____

12 circulation _____

B   **Write the correct word or phrase from exercise 1A next to each definition.**

1 _____ body parts, such as the lungs and the heart, that are inside the body

2 _____ a network of cells and tissues that fight infection and disease in the body

3 _____ the movement of blood inside the body

4 _____ a way of living involving little or no physical activity

5 _____ an illness of the heart and blood vessels

6 _____ a constant ache

7 _____ the body's ability to process food

8 _____ measures of the fatty substance that is found in the blood

9 _____ the force at which the blood moves through the body

10 _____ unwanted results of something

11 _____ places in the body where two bones come together

12 _____ the way that someone holds their body when standing, sitting, or walking

### 2 GRAMMAR: Referencing

A   **Write *P* for pronoun, *PA* for possessive adjective, or *AV* for auxiliary verb next to each word.**

1 their ___

2 were ___

3 this ___

4 they ___

5 does ___

6 its ___

**B** (Circle) the correct words and phrases to complete the paragraphs.

Do you eat healthy food and exercise regularly in order to have a healthy lifestyle? Even if you ¹*do / have / are*, there is one important aspect of your health that you might not think about—your posture. Poor posture makes your body work harder than it needs to, and ²*you / they / this* can result in serious consequences for the body, such as back pain and muscle aches. Good posture, on the other hand, allows you to use your muscles efficiently and helps ensure that ³*it / they / their* remain healthy as you grow older.

If you feel that you have bad posture, there are several ways that you can improve ⁴*them / your / it*. Exercises can strengthen your back and shoulders to help you sit and stand taller. Specific stretching exercises can have ⁵*the same / similar results / them*. Posture correctors can also help. ⁶*They / It / Their* are usually worn around the chest and shoulders, holding the back straight and the shoulders back. These days, you can even use an app to improve your posture. Some apps simply send you reminders to take a break to stand up, stretch, and check your posture. ⁷*Some / Them / One* uses a webcam to monitor your posture and tells you to improve it. Apps that use your phone or a sensor attached to your back do ⁸*similar results / it / the same*.

## 3 GRAMMAR AND VOCABULARY

**A** **Add another sentence using the cues in parentheses and your own ideas. Do research if necessary.**

1 Taking a walk after a big meal can help your digestion. (do the same)

_____

2 Drinking a lot of water helps improve circulation. (similar results)

_____

3 Some people have a very sedentary lifestyle. (they, their)

_____

4 Sugary sodas are not beneficial to the immune system. (are)

_____

5 People often have bad posture at their desks or when looking at their phones. (this)

_____

# 9.2 A GOOD NIGHT'S SLEEP

## 1 VOCABULARY: Discussing (lack of) sleep (phrasal verbs)

A **Circle the correct word to complete each phrasal verb.**

| | | | |
|---|---|---|---|
| 1 add ______ | up | out | away |
| 2 rack ______ | in | off | up |
| 3 pack something ______ something | into | over | up |
| 4 build ______ | into | down | up |
| 5 cut back ______ something | up | into | on |
| 6 cut ______ something | in | out | over |
| 7 drift ______ | of | within | off |
| 8 fit something ______ something | up | into | of |
| 9 wind ______ | down | over | off |
| 10 drive somebody ______ something | at | to | of |
| 11 slip ______ | to | away | from |
| 12 keep somebody ______ | at | to | up |

B **Complete the sentences with the correct forms of the phrasal verbs from exercise 1A.**

1 I have so much to do that it's difficult for me to __fit__ seven or eight hours of sleep __into__ my day.
2 Reading a book helps me to ______ and relax after a stressful day.
3 I went to bed early last night and actually managed to ______ eight hours of sleep.
4 I'm trying to ______ sugar from my diet, so I don't drink or eat anything with sugar in it.
5 I feel like I just got to work, but I've been here for six hours already. Time just ______.
6 I tried to stay awake during the movie, but I was so tired that I ______.
7 If you don't deal with stress right away, it will just ______ and get worse.
8 I have eight meetings today! I don't think I can ______ anything else ______ my day.
9 My neighbor's loud music ______ me ______ all night.
10 You should ______ caffeine. Try to have just one cup of coffee a day.
11 My stressful job ______ me ______ go to the gym every evening. Working out helps me de-stress.
12 I was going to take a short nap, but the minutes ______ to hours and I slept half the day.

## 2 GRAMMAR: Continuous infinitives

A **Correct the mistakes in the sentences.**

1 He seems to ^be^ spending a lot of time online.

2 You should to be sleeping, not watching movies all night long.

3 For the next two nights, I'm going to be sleep in the living room because I just painted my bedroom.

4 You might to be sleeping badly because there's too much light in your bedroom.

5 I'd like to living in a quieter neighborhood by this time next year.

6 They appear asking people about their sleep habits.

B **Write sentences with continuous infinitives. Use the cues in parentheses.**

1 (teenagers / should / sleep / eight to ten hours a night)

_____

2 (six-year-olds / need / get / ten to eleven hours of sleep each night)

_____

3 (my son / might / not / sleep / enough)

_____

4 (she / appear / stay up / too late every night)

_____

5 (you / could / drink / too much coffee during the day)

_____

6 (the baby / seem / wake up now)

_____

## 3 GRAMMAR AND VOCABULARY

A **Read the letter from "Not Sleeping" and write a response using continuous infinitives and the cues in parentheses.**

### ADVICE FROM MS. WISDOM

Dear Ms. Wisdom,

I'm tired all the time, and I'm not sure what to do. I wake up at 6 a.m. every morning and go to the gym for an hour. Then I take a shower and go to school. I have classes until noon, and then I work from 1:00 to 5:00. I get home at around 5:30 and I have dinner. Then I study for a few hours. At about 10:00, I go to bed and spend a couple of hours looking at social media posts or watching TV. I try to go to sleep around midnight, but I have trouble falling asleep.

So tired,

Not Sleeping

1 (comment on ongoing action with *pack into* and *appear* or *seem*)

_____

2 (comment on intentions or plans with *cut back on* and *need*)

_____

3 (speculate with *keep up* and *could* or *might*)

_____

4 (criticize with *wind down* and *should*)

_____

## 1 LISTENING

A 🔊 9.01 **LISTEN FOR PURPOSE** Listen to an interview with two candidates for mayor of Barton and answer the questions.

1 Is Karen Green interested in finding solutions to the water quality issues?    **Yes**   **No**
2 Is Michael Lee interested in finding solutions to the water quality issues?    **Yes**   **No**
3 Is the interviewer satisfied with Karen Green's answers?    **Yes**   **No**
4 Is the interviewer satisfied with Michael Lee's answers?    **Yes**   **No**

B 🔊 9.01 **LISTEN FOR PURPOSE** Listen again and check (✓) the phrases and sentences you hear.

1 Wouldn't you agree that this is an issue that deserves attention? ☐
2 Are you suggesting that … is not an issue? ☐
3 Well, that's certainly an interesting claim, but I'd like to see some facts to back that up. ☐
4 Isn't it fair to say that the situation is critical? ☐
5 I'll have to get back to you on that. ☐
6 Well, that's an interesting point … . ☐
7 Don't you think it's time …? ☐
8 How do you explain the fact that …? ☐
9 How exactly are you proposing to do that …? ☐
10 I'm afraid I can't comment on the issue at the moment. ☐

C 🔊 9.02 **LISTEN FOR STRESSED AND UNSTRESSED GRAMMAR WORDS** Listen to the sentences from the interview. **Underline** the complex noun phrase in each sentence. (Circle) the word with the main stress.

1 Residents of the city of Barton want clean water.
2 Their fear of drinking contaminated water has driven them to rely on bottled water for drinking and cooking.
3 Several studies illustrating Barton's growing water pollution problem have been published in the local newspaper, Ms. Green.
4 These experts in water pollution and safety will be able to help me design a plan to clean up our water supply.
5 If I am elected mayor, a committee consisting of some of these experts, local engineers, and city employees will take action to make sure that our residents have clean water to drink.

## 2 CRITICAL THINKING

A **THINK CRITICALLY** What are two possible reasons that one of the mayoral candidates does not give straight answers to the interviewer's questions?

1 _____

2 _____

## 3 SPEAKING

A **Number the conversation in order.**

| | | |
|---|---|---|
| ___ | **Mayor** | Well, that's certainly an interesting claim, but I'd like to see some facts to back that up. I haven't seen any proof that landlords are asking for twice as much money. |
| ___ | **Interviewer** | This city is growing fast, and because so many people are looking for apartments, some landlords are charging double the usual rent. |
| ___ | **Interviewer** | How do you explain the fact that long-time residents are moving to neighboring cities to find housing? |
| ___ | **Interviewer** | Some of these long-time residents are taking their businesses with them when they move. We've already lost ten percent of our local businesses. Are you suggesting that that is not an issue? |
| 1 | **Interviewer** | Don't you think maybe it's a good idea to talk about the housing prices in this city? |
| ___ | **Mayor** | I'll need to get back to you on that after I've done some research on local businesses. |
| ___ | **Mayor** | I'm glad you brought that up. We certainly are looking into housing prices. |
| ___ | **Mayor** | Well, I'm afraid I can't comment on that. It may be that they prefer the other cities. |

B **Imagine that a lot of cars are suddenly being stolen in your city. Write an interview with a police officer. The police officer does not know all the details and isn't ready to give straight answers. Use probing questions and phrases to deflect or buy time to think.**

**Interviewer** _____

_____

**Police officer** _____

_____

**Interviewer** _____

_____

**Police officer** _____

_____

**Interviewer** _____

_____

**Police officer** _____

_____

**Interviewer** _____

_____

**Police officer** _____

_____

# A THIRSTY WORLD

## 1 READING

A **IDENTIFY PURPOSE** **Read the article. Does the writer seem to have an emotional connection to the story?** <u>Underline</u> one sentence that supports your answer.

### Feeding a Hungry World

World hunger is one of the major challenges we face today. It is estimated that nearly eleven percent of the population is underfed. Although there are almost eight billion people on the planet, and experts predict that there will be more than ten billion by the year 2100, the problem is not with the food supply per se. Globally, we produce more than enough food to feed everyone. However, that food is not getting to hundreds of millions of people around the world.

So what, then, is the cause of the food crisis? The main contributing factor in world hunger is poverty. Nearly one billion people live under the poverty line, meaning they have less than $1.90 to spend a day. Consider that the next time you spend $5 on a cup of coffee. Many people, particularly people in developing countries, simply cannot afford to buy nutritious food. In addition, poverty by its very nature creates more poverty. As a matter of course, poverty leads to hunger and malnutrition, which leads to illness, physical weakness, and mental exhaustion. As such, malnourished people don't have the ability or the energy to work and earn money, so the cycle of poverty continues. Financial donations help, but they can't solve the problem, which, fundamentally, is the lack of regular access to healthy food.

An organization called Groundswell International is attempting to solve the world hunger crisis by providing that access, one community at a time … .

B **Write answers to the questions.**

1 Globally, how many people don't have enough food?

_____

2 How high will the global population get by the year 2100?

_____

3 How many people live under the poverty line?

_____

4 What is the poverty line in dollars per day?

_____

## 2 CRITICAL THINKING

A **THINK CRITICALLY** **Answer the questions.**

1 What do you think might be another cause of world hunger?

_____

2 What is one way that you could contribute to a solution to hunger in your own community?

_____

## 3 WRITING

**A** (Circle) the correct adverbials to complete the paragraph.

Community, [1]*by definition / as such / per se*, is a group of people who live together in the same place. [2]*In and of itself / Per se / As such*, members of a community should help each other. It has come to my attention that many elderly people in this community don't have access to good food. The local food bank has groceries for people in need, but this won't solve the problem [3]*by definition / in and of itself / by its very nature*. [4]*Fundamentally / As a matter of course / As such*, the issue is that the majority of our elderly residents are unable to get to the food bank or the supermarket to get groceries. The majority of them are also unable to prepare food for themselves, so [5]*by its very nature / at its heart / as a matter of course*, they don't get the nourishment that they need.

**B** **Groundswell International is an organization that provides people with the resources to produce their own food. Read the information about the organization and write an explanatory paragraph about how it helps solve the world hunger crisis.**

Groundswell International teaches family farmers how to:

- improve and regenerate their soil
- harvest rainwater for farming
- improve their seed supplies

The family farmers are able to:

- grow food for their families and their community
- earn money from farming
- send their children to school

---
---
---
---
---
---

# CHECK AND REVIEW

**Read the statements. Can you do these things?**

| UNIT 9 | Mark the boxes. ✔ I can do it. ? I am not sure.<br>I can … | If you are not sure, go back to these pages in the Student's Book. |
|---|---|---|
| VOCABULARY | ☐ discuss health issues.<br>☐ discuss (lack of) sleep (phrasal verbs). | page 86<br>page 88 |
| GRAMMAR | ☐ use referencing techniques.<br>☐ use continuous infinitives. | page 87<br>page 89 |
| LISTENING AND SPEAKING SKILLS | ☐ listen for purpose in an interview.<br>☐ ask probing questions, buy time to think, and deflect. | page 90<br>page 91 |
| READING AND WRITING SKILLS | ☐ identify purpose in an article.<br>☐ write an explanatory paragraph. | page 92<br>page 93 |

## 1 VOCABULARY: Discussing global food issues

A Find the words from the box in the word search.

| appetite | cattle | cereal | consumption | fiber |
| foodstuffs | grain | livestock | nutritious | shortage |
| superfood | supply | wholesome | | |

| S | P | O | G | R | C | F | O | F | O | O | S | A | F | G | F | O | N | S | E | L | A | G |
|---|---|---|---|---|---|---|---|---|---|---|---|---|---|---|---|---|---|---|---|---|---|---|
| E | A | N | C | R | A | W | A | B | L | A | D | N | R | S | W | G | F | I | B | E | R | O |
| S | G | U | T | S | H | O | R | T | A | G | E | C | V | E | R | R | S | B | W | S | I | R |
| T | A | T | E | W | S | E | O | B | S | A | R | N | F | O | R | A | C | F | K | A | N | G |
| L | C | R | S | H | I | W | P | A | U | G | I | A | T | T | L | I | U | T | G | A | D | V |
| F | K | I | B | O | K | C | O | N | S | U | M | P | T | I | O | N | V | X | C | G | B | N |
| W | S | T | N | L | F | E | D | S | Y | S | U | P | E | R | F | O | O | D | R | S | M | O |
| G | A | I | V | E | N | O | G | T | A | O | N | E | K | G | O | B | I | H | L | Z | E | U |
| F | O | O | D | S | T | U | F | F | S | F | W | T | C | O | A | C | E | N | M | O | E | N |
| D | C | U | L | O | S | U | O | M | U | I | F | I | A | L | I | V | E | S | T | O | C | K |
| T | U | S | D | M | B | W | O | T | P | C | S | T | E | D | B | N | R | W | A | I | H | L |
| O | K | V | T | E | C | R | N | G | P | H | C | E | R | E | A | L | O | K | G | Y | R | I |
| N | R | C | A | T | T | L | E | B | L | C | L | I | S | P | P | N | W | C | A | N | O | P |
| V | F | B | A | D | M | W | D | X | Y | K | M | L | C | G | I | N | U | C | N | T | N | H |
| L | P | B | W | S | S | I | H | F | Y | S | A | R | N | R | N | O | L | T | E | M | U | A |

B Write the correct word from exercise 1A next to each definition.

1 farm animals, such as cows, pigs, and chickens _____

2 the process of using or eating something so that it no longer exists _____

3 a seed from a plant, such as wheat _____

4 a food that is thought to be good for your health in many ways _____

5 an amount of something that is available for use _____

6 a lack of something that is wanted or needed _____

7 a desire to eat something _____

8 containing vitamins and minerals and other things your body needs _____

9 anything used as food _____

## 2 GRAMMAR: Simple past for unreal situations

A **Read the sentences. Write A (has already happened) or W (the speaker would like to happen).**

1 A company called Beyond Meat created a meat alternative that tastes like meat. ___

2 It's time we all tried different meat alternatives. ___

3 I tried a shrimp alternative made from pea protein and other ingredients. ___

4 Some people would rather we never started raising cows for beef. ___

5 What if someone created a meat alternative that tasted better than beef? ___

6 Imagine if you could create your own meat out of vegetables. ___

B **Rewrite the sentences to use the simple past and the phrases in parentheses.**

1 People should start eating less meat. (It's time)

_____

2 Maybe we can make meat in a laboratory. (What if we)

_____

3 It's urgent that we find a better food source. (It's high time)

_____

4 Picture this—we eat only bugs. (Imagine if)

_____

5 Some people prefer that we find an alternative to eating meat. (would rather)

_____

6 Can you imagine not eating meat for the rest of your life? (Imagine if you)

_____

7 It's urgent that we make changes to protect the environment. (It's high time)

_____

## 3 GRAMMAR AND VOCABULARY

A **Complete the sentences with the cues in parentheses and your own ideas. Do research if necessary.**

1 Imagine if (supply)

_____

2 What if (grains)

_____

3 Vegetarians would rather (appetite)

_____

4 It's time (consumption)

_____

5 It's high time (superfoods)

_____

## 2 GRAMMAR: *It* constructions

**A** **Correct the mistakes in the sentences.**

1 It is believe that solar power can be a source of energy almost anywhere.

2 Is reported that over 100 cities are powered by at least 70% renewable energy.

3 It would seems that these cities have found reliable alternatives to fossil fuels.

4 It would appeared that many other cities are willing to try switching to renewable energy sources.

5 It claim that we will run out of oil by around 2070.

6 It was appear that we need to find an alternative to oil sooner than later.

**B** **Write sentences with the cues in parentheses.**

1 (it / seem / solar power / one good alternative to fossil fuels)

2 (it / report / we may not / able to rely / on solar energy alone)

3 (it / appear / solar energy / not 100% reliable)

4 (it / believe / best solution / to use multiple sources / renewable energy)

5 (it / hope / we / find / more alternative energy sources)

6 (it / claim / fossil fuels / soon disappear)

## 3 GRAMMAR AND VOCABULARY

**A** **Write sentences using the phrase from Column A and the word from Column B. Do research if necessary.**

| | Column A | Column B |
|---|---|---|
| 1 | It is believed | renewable |
| 2 | It is reported | carbon footprints |
| 3 | It would seem | low-emission |
| 4 | It would appear | power |
| 5 | It is hoped | fossil fuels |

# A LIFE WITHOUT PLASTIC

## 1 LISTENING

A 🔊 **10.01** **DISTINGUISH MAIN IDEAS FROM DETAILS** Look at the topics. Circle the two that you think are main ideas. Then listen to Carla and Max's conversation and check your answers.

a We should produce less garbage.

b We should not buy packaged foods.

c You can limit yourself to one jar of garbage for the year.

d You can buy milk in recyclable glass jars.

e We should use less plastic.

f You can just recycle your plastic.

g A lot of plastic doesn't get recycled.

h Plastic hurts marine life.

i There is an island of plastic in the ocean.

j Energy drinks come in plastic bottles.

k Limiting your garbage production makes you think about what you're buying.

l Limiting your garbage production makes you eat better.

B 🔊 **10.01** **LISTEN FOR DETAILS** Listen again. Which points does Carla make and which ones does Max make? Check the correct column.

|  | Carla | Max |
|---|---|---|
| 1 We should produce less garbage. | ☐ | ☐ |
| 2 We should not buy packaged foods. | ☐ | ☐ |
| 3 You can limit yourself to one jar of garbage for the year. | ☐ | ☐ |
| 4 You can buy milk in recyclable glass jars. | ☐ | ☐ |
| 5 We should use less plastic. | ☐ | ☐ |
| 6 You can just recycle your plastic. | ☐ | ☐ |
| 7 A lot of plastic doesn't get recycled. | ☐ | ☐ |
| 8 Plastic hurts marine life. | ☐ | ☐ |
| 9 There is an island of plastic in the ocean. | ☐ | ☐ |
| 10 Energy drinks come in plastic bottles. | ☐ | ☐ |
| 11 Limiting your garbage production makes you think about what you're buying. | ☐ | ☐ |
| 12 Limiting your garbage production makes you eat better. | ☐ | ☐ |

## 2 CRITICAL THINKING

A **THINK CRITICALLY** Why do you think some people are resistant to switching from fossil fuels to renewable energy?

_____

_____

_____

_____

SPEAKING

A   Complete the sentences with the phrases from the box.

| | | |
|---|---|---|
| all I'm saying | as simple as that | comes down to |
| so much more that | that difficult | point I'm trying to make |

1   A lot of people recycle and drive low-emission cars, but there's _____ can be done.

2   You can reduce your plastic waste. I mean, it's not _____ .

3   You can take public transportation instead of driving in order to reduce your carbon footprint, but it's not

_____ .

4   Just try buying fewer foods that are packaged in plastic. That's _____ .

5   It all _____ being aware of your how big your carbon footprint is.

6   We don't need to use plastic bags for our produce. That's the _____ .

B   Imagine that your friend is telling you that solar panels are the best way to reduce your carbon footprint. Write a conversation about it and disagree with your friend. Use expressions for defending your opinion and concluding a turn.

Your friend   I think putting solar panels on my house is the best way to reduce my carbon footprint.

You   _____

_____

Your friend   _____

_____

You   _____

_____

Your friend   _____

_____

You   _____

_____

Your friend   _____

_____

## 1 READING

**A** Before you read, what do you think of peer-to-peer car sharing, in which individuals rent their cars out to people when they're not using them? (Circle) your answer.

It's a good idea.     It's a bad idea.

**B** **PREDICT FROM CONTENT** Look at the key words and phrases related to the discussion thread below. Which do you think will be used to defend peer-to-peer car sharing and which will be used to criticize it? Write *D* (defend) or *C* (criticize). Read the thread and check your answers.

1 financial risk ___
2 increased insurance rates ___
3 great alternative ___
4 financial rewards ___
5 subsidize ___
6 acceptable risk ___

### Peer-to-Peer Car Sharing—Good or Bad?

With the rise of the sharing economy, anyone can earn money by sharing their knowledge, their homes, and their work spaces. What do you think about peer-to-peer car sharing?

**A**  **Joseph**

At first glance it would seem that renting out your car when you're not using it is an easy way to make some extra money. However, with respect to the financial aspect of peer-to-peer car sharing, you could be taking a big financial risk. What if the driver gets into an accident? Would you be facing increased insurance rates? Who would be responsible for paying for any damage caused? In brief, I think this kind of car sharing is a bad idea.

**B**  **Zarina**

Regarding the risks and rewards of peer-to-peer car sharing, I think the financial rewards far outweigh the risks. Car owners can earn more than $10 an hour in some places. Rent your car out for ten hours a week, and you're bringing in an extra $400 a month. By no means am I suggesting that you should participate if you feel uncomfortable doing so. For some, however, it is a great way to subsidize the cost of a car.

**C**  **Miguel**

It's probably true that there is a certain level of acceptable risk when renting a car out to strangers. From the perspective of a car renter, though, peer-to-peer car sharing is a great alternative to buying a car or renting one from a rental agency. Wouldn't you rather pay a few dollars to rent a car for an hour than pay for a whole day when you don't need it that long?

**C** **IDENTIFY MAIN POINTS AND OPINION** Read the thread again. Match the contributors to the main points they make. Then (circle) the names of the contributors who are in favor of peer-to-peer car sharing.

1 Joseph ___
2 Zarina ___
3 Miguel ___

a It's a great way to make extra money.
b It's too big of a financial risk.
c It's a good alternative to renting from an agency.

## 2 CRITICAL THINKING

**A** **THINK CRITICALLY** Which of the opinions in the discussion thread do you agree with? Why? Has your opinion changed about the topic? If so, in what way?

_____

_____

## 3 WRITING

A   Which phrases can complete the sentences? Write the phrases from the box in the correct places in the chart.

| by no means | even if you wouldn't | in a nutshell, | in brief, |
| in terms of | in this respect, | it would seem | not at all |
| regarding | regardless of whether you would | with respect to | |

| | |
|---|---|
| 1 _____ peer-to-peer car sharing rewards both car owners and car renters. | _____ <br> _____ <br> _____ |
| 2 _____ like to participate, it's a good idea in general. | _____ |
| 3 _____ accidents, you should make sure you have a good insurance plan. | _____ <br> _____ <br> _____ |
| 4 Peer-to-peer car sharing is _____ a solution for everyone. | _____ <br> _____ |

B   Write a formal summary of the discussion thread, focusing on the positive viewpoints. Use the expressions in exercise 3A where possible.

_____

_____

_____

_____

# CHECK AND REVIEW

Read the statements. Can you do these things?

| UNIT 10 | Mark the boxes.  ✔ I can do it.   ? I am not sure. <br><br> I can … | If you are not sure, go back to these pages in the Student's Book. |
|---|---|---|
| VOCABULARY | ☐ discuss global food issues. <br> ☐ discuss global energy issues. | page 98 <br> page 100 |
| GRAMMAR | ☐ use the simple past to talk about unreal situations. <br> ☐ use *it* constructions. | page 99 <br> page 101 |
| LISTENING AND SPEAKING SKILLS | ☐ distinguish main ideas from details in a conversation. <br> ☐ use expressions for defending an opinion and concluding a turn. | page 102 <br> page 103 |
| READING AND WRITING SKILLS | ☐ identify opinions and main points in a discussion thread. <br> ☐ write a formal summary of a discussion thread. | page 105 <br> page 105 |

## 11.1  THE COLOR COMPANY

**1** VOCABULARY: Describing color associations

A  **Write each word or phrase in the correct place in the chart.**

| bold | capture | conjure up | convey | evoke | imply | muted |
| neutral | pastel | reflect | resonate with | saturated | transmit | vibrant |

| Verbs used for color associations | Adjectives that describe colors |
|---|---|
|  |  |

B  **Write the correct word from exercise 1A next to each definition. You won't use all the words.**

1  bright: _____

2  suggest: _____

3  perfectly represent an idea or feeling: _____

4  used to describe shades like gray, brown, white, black, or beige: _____

5  not bright: _____

6  accurately represent something that is happening: _____

7  completely full of color: _____

## 2 GRAMMAR: Subject–verb agreement

A  Write S (singular verb), P (plural verb), or B (both) next to each subject.

1  The company ___
2  Data ___
3  No one ___
4  Criteria ___
5  Physics ___
6  The team ___
7  The employees at Pantone ___
8  Neither ___
9  Everyone ___
10  News ___

B  Use the cues in parentheses to write sentences. Include a pronoun or a possessive adjective where necessary.

1  (Pantone / have / over 10,000 colors / in / color library)
   Pantone has over 10,000 colors in its color library.

2  (The criteria for choosing a color / include / the feelings it / evoke)
   _____

3  (Either of these two colors / be / a good choice for our logo)
   _____

4  (The news about Pantone's color of the year / be / surprising)
   _____

5  (Everyone / using / the color of the year in / products / right now)
   _____

6  (Neither of these colors / work / because / too muted)
   _____

7  (Right now, the team / working / on choosing a color for next year)
   _____

8  (Pantone employees / be / experts in color theory)
   _____

## 3 GRAMMAR AND VOCABULARY

A  Pick a color from Column A and a color association verb from Column B. Make sentences with your own ideas.

| Column A | Column B |
| --- | --- |
| green | conjure up |
| blue | capture |
| red | evoke |
| yellow | convey |
| black | reflect |

1  _____
2  _____
3  _____
4  _____
5  _____

**1** VOCABULARY: Color expressions

A   **Match each expression with its meaning.**

| | | |
|---|---|---|
| 1 caught red-handed _____ | a | owing money |
| 2 in the red _____ | b | get permission to do something |
| 3 see red _____ | c | be good at growing plants |
| 4 cut through red tape _____ | d | young and inexperienced |
| 5 turn red _____ | e | get angry |
| 6 green party _____ | f | be embarrassed |
| 7 have a green thumb _____ | g | an ecological political group |
| 8 get the green light _____ | h | deal with a lot of rules quickly and efficiently |
| 9 green / a greenhorn _____ | i | not feeling well |
| 10 green around the gills _____ | j | found doing something wrong |

B   **Complete the sentences with the phrases in the box.**

| | | |
|---|---|---|
| got the green light | had to cut through a lot of red tape | got caught red-handed |
| green | green around the gills | green party |
| has a green thumb | was seeing red | |

1   Are you feeling OK? You look a little _____ .

2   James _____ stealing money from the cash register.

3   Michael's garden is amazing. He really _____ .

4   I wasn't sure that my boss was going to let us go ahead with our idea, but we
_____ to move forward.

5   Anna was so angry that she _____ .

6   Are you sure Ken can handle the project by himself? He's only been here for a few months and he's still pretty
_____ .

7   I _____ , but I've finally gotten my visa situation sorted out.

8   I usually vote for _____ candidates because I think the environment is
the most important political issue of our time.

## 2 GRAMMAR: Articles

A **Check (✓) the correct sentences. Then correct the mistakes in the incorrect sentences.**

1 ~~A~~ *The* color green conveys many different ideas. ☐

2 The people who are colorblind can't see certain colors, such as blue, yellow, green, or red. ☐

3 We have to choose a color for our company logo. ☐

4 Do you like the color we selected? ☐

5 Daniel is still greenhorn. He isn't ready to lead a team yet. ☐

6 That's most beautiful color I've ever seen. ☐

B **Circle the correct answers to complete the sentences.**

1 Those flowers are *a / the / no article* same shade of purple as my sweater.

2 Did you know that *a / the / no article* purple is my favorite color?

3 I just read that *a / the / no article* yellow is *a / the / no article* color of both *a / the / no article* happiness and *a / the / no article* fearfulness.

4 I just bought *a / the / no article* yellow car.

5 I think this is *a / the / no article* best paint color for *a / the / no article* dining room. It matches *a / the / no article* carpet in there.

6 What *a / the / no article* feeling does *a / the / no article* color red evoke for you?

7 She has *a / the / no article* hair *a / the / no article* color of chocolate.

8 I can't believe that *a / the / no article* Pantone has so many shades of *a / the / no article* white.

## 3 GRAMMAR AND VOCABULARY

A **Write sentences using the expressions in parentheses and your own ideas. Be sure to include articles when necessary.**

1 (a green thumb)

_____

2 (turn red)

_____

3 (caught red-handed)

_____

4 (green around the gills)

_____

5 (get the green light)

_____

6 (in the red)

_____

7 (green)

_____

8 (see red)

_____

# 11.3 IT TASTES LIKE GREEN!

## 1 LISTENING

A 🔊 **11.01** **LISTEN FOR MAIN POINTS** Listen to the class discussion about food and color. What is the topic of the discussion?

a Colorful foods are good for your health.

b Certain colors represent different nutrients contained in foods.

c The color of food can affect whether or not you want to eat it.

B 🔊 **11.01** **LISTEN FOR DETAILS** Listen again. According to the class discussion, what feelings does each color evoke in relation to food? Write notes in the chart.

| Topic | Details |
|-------|---------|
| Blue | |
| Red | |
| Green | |
| Yellow | |
| Orange | |

SPEAKING

A **Match 1–12 with a–l to make complete responses.**

1 Well, the short answer    _c_           a understand that.

2 Perhaps I can answer   _____        b by that exactly?

3 Would you like to      _____        c is yes.

4 Sorry, I'm not sure I    _____       d Could you rephrase the question, please?

5 That's a             _____       e I've understood your question.

6 Well, I've never really   _____    f take this one?

7 I'm afraid that's not     _____     g have to say …

8 Sorry, what do you mean   _____  h good question.

9 I guess I would       _____       i really my area.

10 I'm glad             _____       j that one.

11 I'm not sure I understand.  _____  k you asked that.

12 Sorry, let me just check   _____  l thought about it like that.

B **Complete the questions and write responses about the reasons that certain colors are used, or not used, for certain products. Use the responses in exercise 2A and your own ideas.**

A Why do you think soda companies _____

_____ ?

B _____

_____

A Why do you think car companies _____

_____ ?

B _____

_____

A Why do you think computer companies _____

_____ ?

B _____

_____

# A SENSE OF IDENTITY

## 1 READING

A **EVALUATE INFORMATION** Read the article and write notes in the chart below.

| Soccer team's name | |
|---|---|
| Soccer team's colors | |

### OPINIONS: The New Soccer Team

Our brand-new local soccer team has just chosen its name and colors, and I have to confess that I'm unimpressed by the team's choices. The name the team has chosen is The Dunes, which refers to the sand dunes along the beaches of our town. A lot of locales around town use "the dunes" in their names. For example, our local shopping mall is called "Shops at the Dunes," and there's a hotel by the beach called "The Dunes Inn." I think that the phrase "the dunes" works really well for the mall and the hotel because it conveys the idea of a relaxing beach, but I don't think it's a good name for a sports team. A soccer team should be fast and energetic, and the concept of dunes does not convey speed or energy. Dunes don't move. They just sit there.

The team has chosen the colors blue and brown for their uniforms. These colors represent the ocean and the sand. In my opinion, this is another poor decision. The light and bright shade of blue that was chosen is beautiful, but it evokes feelings of peace rather than energy. The light brown shade that is used in the uniforms doesn't resonate with me at all. It's just a dull, muted color. It doesn't convey energy or speed in any way.

I wish that the team had consulted with city residents before making a final decision about its name and colors. Many people around town are unhappy with the choices. Some, including me, have even written letters to the team, asking them to reconsider their decisions.

## 2 CRITICAL THINKING

A **THINK CRITICALLY** Think about a famous sports team. What is the team's name? What is its symbol or mascot? What are its colors? What do these things convey to you? Do you think they are good choices?

_____

_____

_____

## 3 WRITING

A   Read the article in exercise 1A again. Then complete the chart.

| What opinions does the writer offer? | What examples does the writer give to support those opinions? |
|---|---|
|  |  |
|  |  |

B   **Write an opinion essay on the topic below. Use examples to support your opinion.**

Topic: Imagine that your city is going to have a new baseball team. What colors do you think the team should use? What should the team's name and mascot be?

_____

_____

_____

_____

_____

_____

_____

_____

_____

# CHECK AND REVIEW

**Read the statements. Can you do these things?**

| UNIT 11 | Mark the boxes.   ☑ I can do it.   ❓ I am not sure.   I can … | If you are not sure, go back to these pages in the Student's Book. |
|---|---|---|
| VOCABULARY | ☐ describe color associations.<br>☐ use color expressions. | page 108<br>page 110 |
| GRAMMAR | ☐ use verbs that agree with their subjects.<br>☐ use articles correctly. | page 109<br>page 111 |
| LISTENING AND SPEAKING SKILLS | ☐ listen for uncertainty in a discussion.<br>☐ respond to questions for different purposes. | page 112<br>page 113 |
| READING AND WRITING SKILLS | ☐ read an article and take notes.<br>☐ write an opinion essay. | page 115<br>page 115 |

### 1 VOCABULARY: Talking about change

A **Match each word with its synonym.**

| | | | | |
|---|---|---|---|---|
| 1 | embrace | ____ | a | change |
| 2 | disruption | ____ | b | adjustment |
| 3 | transition | ____ | c | interrupting |
| 4 | implement | ____ | d | accept |
| 5 | disruptive | ____ | e | a shake-up |
| 6 | innovative | ____ | f | go through |
| 7 | innovation | ____ | g | opposition |
| 8 | adaptation | ____ | h | facilitate |
| 9 | resistance | ____ | i | invention |
| 10 | undergo | ____ | j | inventive |

B **Circle the correct word to complete each sentence.**

1 Big changes often face a lot of *disruption / transition / resistance* from people who are uncomfortable with change.

2 My company has been *undergoing / disrupting / innovating* a lot of changes lately, such as new management and a bigger office.

3 Change is often beneficial, but it can be *innovative / adaptable / disruptive* at the beginning.

4 Some people are having a difficult time with the *resistance / shake-up / innovation* to their regular routines.

5 The ability to deal with *resistance / facilitation / transition* is an important quality in this day and age because things change very fast.

6 I really like your ideas for changes to the company, but I'm not sure how we can *disrupt / undergo / implement* them without upsetting our clients.

7 We've come up with some *disruptive / innovative / resistant* strategies to improve our business.

8 I'm finding it difficult to *transition / embrace / facilitation* these changes because I don't agree with many of them.

## 2 GRAMMAR: The present subjunctive

A **Correct the mistakes in the sentences.**

1 The company insisted that employees are prepared to change offices at any time.

2 The management recommends that each employee becomes familiar with the new plan.

3 The suggestion that we are open to any upcoming changes is a good one.

4 It is crucial that the change goes as smoothly as possible.

5 I ask that everyone works together to implement this change as quickly as possible.

B **Use the words from the box and the cues in parentheses to write sentences with the subjunctive.**

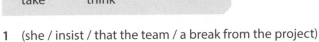

| be | happen | listen |
|----|--------|--------|
| take | think | |

1 (she / insist / that the team / a break from the project)

_____

2 (I / suggest / that you / ready for anything)

_____

3 (my recommendation / be / that everyone / carefully before making a decision)

_____

4 (it / be / imperative / that the changes / slowly)

_____

5 (they / request / that we / to the whole plan before asking questions)

_____

## 3 GRAMMAR AND VOCABULARY

A **Imagine that you are giving advice to a friend who is having difficulty dealing with changes at work. Complete each sentence with a word from the box and your own ideas. Use the subjunctive.**

| embrace | transition | resistance | disruptive |
|---------|-----------|------------|-----------|
| a shake-up | innovative | implement | adaptation |

1 It is crucial that _____

_____ .

2 I suggest that _____

_____ .

3 My recommendation is that _____

_____ .

4 It's important that _____

_____ .

5 You can request that _____

_____ .

# WHAT ON EARTH?

## 1 VOCABULARY: Describing change

**A Find the words from the box.**

| | | | | |
|---|---|---|---|---|
| abrupt | desired | drastic | fundamental | gradual |
| lasting | profound | radical | refreshing | subtle |
| sweeping | unforeseen | welcome | | |

| | | | | | | | | | | | | | | | | | | | | | | |
|---|---|---|---|---|---|---|---|---|---|---|---|---|---|---|---|---|---|---|---|---|---|---|
| R | C | A | F | U | T | P | O | I | M | A | E | D | H | U | N | J | F | O | C | F | T | O |
| X | L | F | P | B | S | K | T | D | G | D | R | J | U | S | A | B | M | M | C | H | I | K |
| I | E | R | A | D | I | C | A | L | L | U | L | T | H | S | S | U | A | M | V | G | P | L |
| A | T | O | M | E | D | F | S | P | E | E | C | G | R | A | D | U | A | L | H | Q | M | U |
| A | K | G | X | S | B | F | R | I | A | J | F | K | Q | B | N | A | P | I | P | O | R | N |
| U | Q | J | I | I | T | U | L | C | X | R | V | G | C | R | E | T | U | D | D | K | S | T |
| L | O | D | E | R | O | N | G | O | H | O | U | N | I | U | U | A | N | M | P | H | U | D |
| S | H | R | C | E | E | D | W | E | L | C | O | M | E | P | R | O | F | O | U | N | D | C |
| E | R | A | V | D | R | A | S | T | I | C | A | F | U | T | T | T | O | F | I | P | A | F |
| M | B | I | U | P | M | M | H | P | G | I | U | E | M | G | K | S | R | H | R | A | E | S |
| T | F | I | U | M | R | E | F | R | E | S | H | I | N | G | P | D | S | O | X | G | M | U |
| H | E | K | S | D | O | N | H | K | V | T | U | S | C | O | L | E | E | M | U | K | U | B |
| N | D | X | L | U | U | T | F | U | R | P | I | O | Q | D | O | S | E | T | I | O | D | T |
| I | A | O | R | I | H | A | E | S | M | E | S | W | E | E | P | I | N | G | F | B | U | L |
| D | M | S | N | R | P | L | N | P | Q | B | A | X | H | G | P | L | S | J | E | J | B | E |
| C | I | T | T | X | P | U | D | C | A | E | L | F | L | E | H | I | V | R | A | M | U | P |
| T | U | A | L | A | S | T | I | N | G | I | N | U | T | O | C | J | U | R | I | V | O | S |

**B Cross out the word that doesn't belong.**

1 sweeping    radical    subtle    profound
2 abrupt    sudden    immediate    gradual
3 unforeseen    desired    welcome    refreshing
4 temporary    lasting    continuing    permanent
5 subtle    small    slight    drastic

## 2 GRAMMAR: Perfect infinitive

**A** **Complete each sentence with the perfect infinitive form of the verb in parentheses.**

1 The landscape is reported (change) _____ drastically.

2 We were happy (be able) _____ to have a say in the upcoming transition.

3 They might (find) _____ a better solution to the problem.

4 Everyone seems (adjust) _____ to the recent changes.

5 The change is said (occur) _____ abruptly.

6 I could (help) _____ with the transition.

7 Relocating the entire town to another area appears (work) _____ well.

**B** **Rewrite the sentences to create a sentence with a perfect infinitive.**

1 Someone said that the lake dried up suddenly.
   The lake is said to have dried up suddenly. _____

2 Everyone survived the changes. They were relieved.
   _____

3 Some of the changes had a negative effect. At least that's how it seems.
   _____

4 Someone reported that a river ran through town in the past.
   _____

5 We were sad because we saw so many people leave the town.
   _____

6 Some people think that the city disappeared under lava.
   _____

## 3 GRAMMAR AND VOCABULARY

**A** **Use the words in parentheses and your own ideas to write sentences with the perfect infinitive.**

1 (transition / said) The transition is said to have been gradual. _____

2 (the move / seems) _____

3 (a drastic change / might) _____

4 (we / shocked) _____

5 (everyone / happy) _____

6 (the residents / sad) _____

93

# "AND THAT'S WHEN IT ALL CHANGED!"

## 1 LISTENING

A 🔊 **12.01** **LISTEN FOR MAIN POINTS** Listen to Mila and Luke talk about their friend Carrie. Write short answers to the questions.

1 What does Carrie make? _____

2 How did she get into it? _____

3 How has her life changed? _____

4 Is she happy with the change? _____

B 🔊 **12.01** **LISTEN FOR DETAILS** Listen again and read the statements. Write *T* for true or *F* for false. Then rewrite the false statements to make them true.

1 Mila had coffee with Carrie this morning. ____

_____

2 Luke has seen Carrie's handbags. ____

_____

3 Carrie has been selling her handbags to friends for a while. ____

_____

4 Carrie made a bag for her brother's friend, Margo. ____

_____

5 Margo showed the bag to some friends at a party. ____

_____

6 Carrie was very calm when she started receiving handbag orders. ____

_____

7 Margo's Instagram followers have ordered more than 500 handbags. ____

_____

8 Carrie is making the bags by herself. ____

_____

## 2 CRITICAL THINKING

A **THINK CRITICALLY** What are some reasons that you decide to retell a story that you've heard? When do you choose not to retell a story?

_____

_____

_____

_____

_____

_____

## 3 SPEAKING

A **Complete the expressions with the words from the box. Then write *SD* (skipping details), *RO* (referring to the original), or *SR* (signaling a retelling) next to each expression.**

| | | | | |
|---|---|---|---|---|
| details | exact | rest | speak | story |
| straight | tell | way | what | words |

1  To make a long ___story___ short, …              SD
2  I can't _____ it the way she does.        ____
3  It's much better the _____ she tells it!   ____
4  I got it _____ from the horse's mouth.     ____
5  What were her _____ words?                 ____
6  I can't _____ for her, but …               ____
7  In her own _____ , …                       ____
8  I don't know all the _____ .               ____
9  And the _____ , as they say, is history.   ____
10 Yes, that's _____ she said.                ____

B **Complete the conversations with the expressions in exercise 3A. Several answers may be possible.**

1  A  That's a funny story.
   B  I didn't tell it right, though.
      _____

2  A  Are you sure that's what happened?
   B  _____

3  A  What else did she say?
   B  _____ ,
      she's going to try to be a celebrity impersonator.

4  A  _____
   B  She said, "I have an audition with a celebrity impersonator company."

5  A  Oh, wow. Why does she want to be a celebrity impersonator?
   B  _____ ,
      she thinks she would "make a great Lady Gaga."

C **Think of a story that you've heard recently and imagine that you are retelling it. Complete the sentences with your own ideas.**

1  I don't remember all the details, but _____
   _____ .

2  In his/her own words, _____
   _____ .

3  I can't speak for him/her, but _____
   _____ .

4  To make a long story short, _____
   _____ .

## 1 READING

**A** What is one way that a character can change through the course of a story?

_____

_____

# THREE TYPES OF CHARACTER ARCS

In any story, whether it be told as a movie, a book, or a television series, important characters become different in some way by the end of the story. The process of their change is called a character arc. Character arcs can be broken down into three different categories.

One type of character arc is the transformation arc. With this type of arc, a character essentially becomes a different person by the end of the story. Usually the character starts as an ordinary individual and becomes a hero. An example of this type of character arc is the title character of the _Harry Potter_ series. At the beginning of the series, Harry is a normal boy living an insignificant life, and by the end, he is a hero who saves the world from an evil wizard.

Another type of character arc is the growth arc, which as the name implies, involves a character growing in some way. Less extreme than the transformation arc, this arc might see a character become more mature, learn something new, or develop a new understanding. The title character in the movie _Lady Bird_ follows this type of arc. At the beginning of the film, Lady Bird seems to hate everything about her life, constantly complaining about and rejecting her hometown and her family, particularly her mother, who is difficult to please. As the movie comes to a close, however, Lady Bird begins to accept, and even appreciate, what she has.

The third type of character arc is the fall arc. A character following this arc makes a series of bad choices, and as a result, destroys his or her life by the end of the story. The character of Voldemort in the _Harry Potter_ series is an example of this arc. Resentment over the life he's been given drives him to make bad decisions, which cause him to become less and less human and eventually results in his death.

**B** READ FOR MAIN IDEA According to the writer, what happens in every story?

_____

_____

**C** ANALYZE CONTENT Complete the chart.

| Types of character arc: | The ¹ <u>transformation</u> arc<br><br>Example character:<br>² _____ | The growth arc<br><br>Example character:<br>⁵ _____ | The ⁸ _____ arc<br><br>Example character:<br>Voldemort |
|---|---|---|---|
| At the beginning: | ³ <u>he's a normal boy</u> | ⁶ _____ | ⁹ _____ |
| At the end: | ⁴ _____ | ⁷ _____ | ¹⁰ _____ |

## 2 CRITICAL THINKING

A  **THINK CRITICALLY**  **Think of another movie character that goes through a significant transformation. Who is the character and why does the character change?**

_____

_____

_____

## 3 WRITING

A  **Break this complex sentence into three or more simple sentences. Make any necessary grammatical changes.**

At the beginning of the film, Lady Bird seems to hate everything about her life, constantly complaining about and rejecting her hometown and her family, particularly her mother, who is difficult to please.

_____

_____

_____

B  **In exercise 2A, you wrote about a character from a movie. Now write a review of that movie. Include two or more complex sentences as you explain the plot.**

_____

_____

_____

_____

_____

# CHECK AND REVIEW

**Read the statements. Can you do these things?**

| UNIT 12 | Mark the boxes.  ✔ I can do it.   ? I am not sure. | If you are not sure, go back to these pages in the Student's Book. |
|---|---|---|
| | **I can …** | |
| VOCABULARY | ☐ talk about change. | page 118 |
| | ☐ describe change. | page 120 |
| GRAMMAR | ☐ use the present subjunctive. | page 119 |
| | ☐ use the perfect infinitive. | page 121 |
| LISTENING AND SPEAKING SKILLS | ☐ listen for details in a conversation. | page 122 |
| | ☐ tell a story that I heard from someone else. | page 123 |
| READING AND WRITING SKILLS | ☐ analyze the content of an article. | page 124 |
| | ☐ write a movie review. | page 125 |

## 7.5 TIME TO SPEAK  Preserving a custom

A    Research one of the following cultural celebrations or use your own idea.

> Día de los Muertos, Mexico       Obon, Japan
> Pchum Ben, Cambodia            Gai Jatra, Nepal

B    Find out about how people observe the celebration that you chose. What rites or rituals do they perform? What kinds of foods do they eat? When does the celebration occur?

C    Give a presentation to your class about what you learned.

## 8.5 TIME TO SPEAK  Make a pitch

A    Choose one of the services below. You are going to create an investment pitch for it.

> a restaurant and cooking school where students make all the food
> a company that organizes events to help people make friends
> a hotel where people can stay and take various arts and crafts workshops

B    Identify the key elements of your pitch:
- the strengths, aims, and selling points of your service
- questions people might ask
- the problem(s) that your service will solve
- an analogy that will make the idea accessible
- a mission statement

C    Write your pitch in bullet point format and give a presentation in your next class.

## 9.5 TIME TO SPEAK  Desert island dilemma

A    Imagine that you are going to live on an isolated island for two years with one friend. What are three skills that you think you should learn before you go?

_____

_____

_____

B    Think about the reasons for your choices.

C    Give a presentation in your next class about the three skills that you chose.

## 10.5 TIME TO SPEAK  Rent-a-Pet

A  Imagine that you want to start a business in your community. Choose from the ideas below or use your own idea:

> individuals trade services for handmade goods and vice versa
> people rent out their driveways to people who don't have parking spaces
> people rent out their backyards for parties
> people take turns walking each other's pets
> a community garden that anyone can use

in favor of: _____  _____  _____

against: _____  _____  _____

B  Think of a name for your company and prepare a formal presentation for it. Consider the issues or concerns people may have about your idea.

C  Give a presentation in your next class about your idea.

## 11.5 TIME TO SPEAK  Fly your flag

A  You are responsible for designing new packaging for one of your favorite products. What elements do you need to consider?

_____
_____
_____
_____
_____

B  Choose the three or four most important elements from your list to include in your design. Take notes about the reason for each element and give an example to explain your ideas.

C  Make a drawing of your design.

D  Give a presentation about your new product design in your next class. Bring in the product or a sample of the product to compare to your new design.

## 12.5 TIME TO SPEAK  Every picture tells a story

A  Find a picture online or in a magazine that shows some kind of action and at least two people. You are going to make up a story about it.

B  Decide on the genre of your story and decide who the characters—the people in the picture—are to each other. Then develop the plot and map out your story. Make sure it has a clear beginning, middle, and end, as well as a climax.

C  Bring your picture to your next class and tell your story to your classmates.

The authors and publishers acknowledge the following sources of copyright material and are grateful for the permissions granted. While every effort has been made, it has not always been possible to identify the sources of all the material used, or to trace all copyright holders. If any omissions are brought to our notice, we will be happy to include the appropriate acknowledgments on reprinting and in the next update to the digital edition, as applicable.

**Key:** U = Unit.

**Photographs**
All the photographs are sourced from Getty Images.

**U7:** hadynyah/E+; Amanda V./EyeEm; Arman Rin, Jr./Moment; fstop123/E+; Claudio de Sat/500px; 10'000 Hours/DigitalVision; Ollie Millington/Getty Images Entertainment; **U8:** DGLimages/ iStock/Getty Images Plus; VLG/iStock/Getty Images Plus; Hill Street Studios/DigitalVision; Willie B. Thomas/DigitalVision; Tim Robberts/ DigitalVision; simonkr/E+; **U9:** pattonmania/iStock/Getty Images Plus; IPGGutenbergUKLtd/iStock/Getty Images Plus; Hero Images; alex_ugalek/iStock/Getty Images Plus; kvkirillov/iStock/Getty Images Plus; youngvet/E+; kokouu/iStock/Getty Images Plus; **U10:** aaaaimages/ Moment; SWKrullImaging/iStock/Getty Images Plus; wx-bradwang/E+; Eskay Lim/EyeEm; RusN/iStock/Getty Images Plus; Westend61; **U11:** kasezo/iStock/Getty Images Plus; scanrail/iStock/Getty Images Plus; Kirk Marsh; fotolinchen/E+; LEONELLO CALVETTI/SCIENCE PHOTO LIBRARY; CostinT/E+; Thomas Schelagowski/EyeEm; **U12:** Thomas Gutschlag/EyeEm; Sam Diephuis; Pixelchrome Inc/DigitalVision; olegkalina/iStock/Getty Images Plus; Michael Tran/FilmMagic.

Front cover photography by Hans Neleman/The Image Bank/Getty Images Plus/Getty Images.

Typeset by emc design ltd.

**Audio**
Audio production by CityVox, New York.

**Corpus**
Development of this publication has made use of the Cambridge English Corpus (CEC). The CEC is a multi-billion word collection of contemporary spoken and written English. It includes British English, American English, and other varieties. It also includes the Cambridge Learner Corpus, the world's biggest collection of learner writing, developed in collaboration with Cambridge Assessment. Cambridge University Press uses the CEC to provide evidence about language use that helps to produce better language teaching materials. Our Evolve authors study the Corpus to see how English is really used, and to identify typical learner mistakes. This information informs the authors' selection of vocabulary, grammar items and Student's Book Corpus features such as the Accuracy Check, Register Check, and Insider English.